THE STORY OF AMELIA EARHART

A Biography Book for New Readers

Written by
Stacia Deutsch

Illustrated by
Pearl Law

ROCKRIDGE PRESS

For Rhody, my co-pilot and navigator

I am endlessly awed by Amelia Earhart. I'm not a very brave person, and she was a master at showing courage. Every minute I spent learning about her brought me inspiration. This project is dedicated to the women in my life who show me, by their example, how to be more like Amelia. We all stand on the shoulders of the pioneers who forged the pathways that we now travel. *Incipit vita nova.* Here begins new life.

For general information on our other products and services or to obtain technical support, please contact our Customer Care Department within the United States at (866) 744-2665, or outside the United States at (510) 253-0500.

Rockridge Press publishes its books in a variety of electronic and print formats. Some content that appears in print may not be available in electronic books, and vice versa.

Series Designer: Angela Navarra
Interior and Cover Designer: Angela Navarra
Art Producer: Sue Bischofberger
Editor: Orli Zuravicky
Production Editor: Mia Moran

ISBN: Print 978-1-64739-678-7 | eBook 978-1-64739-417-2

R0

Printed in China

CONTENTS

CHAPTER 1 A Daredevil Is Born 1

CHAPTER 2 The Early Years 7

CHAPTER 3 America's Super Girl 14

CHAPTER 4 Overnight Stardom 21

CHAPTER 5 Amelia Rising 27

CHAPTER 6 Amelia Across the Atlantic 34

CHAPTER 7 Mysterious Disappearance 41

CHAPTER 8 So . . . Who Was Amelia Earhart? 48

GLOSSARY 54

BIBLIOGRAPHY 56

CHAPTER 1

A DAREDEVIL IS BORN

Meet Amelia Earhart

Amelia Earhart was born with a love of adventure. When she was young, Amelia liked to go sledding. One wintry day, she took her sled to the top of a high hill. Instead of sitting on it correctly, Amelia took a running start and belly-flopped onto it. She soared headfirst down the snowy hill and toward the street below. She had no way to turn the sled—and no way to stop.

Suddenly, a horse pulling a carriage walked into the path of Amelia's sled. She closed her eyes. She was going to crash! At the last minute, the horse took a giant step forward. Amelia and her sled slid under the horse's belly. The sled stopped safely on the other side of the street. It was amazing! Amelia jumped up. She couldn't wait to go on another daring adventure.

From the moment Amelia took her first ride in a real airplane in 1920, she was hooked! Over

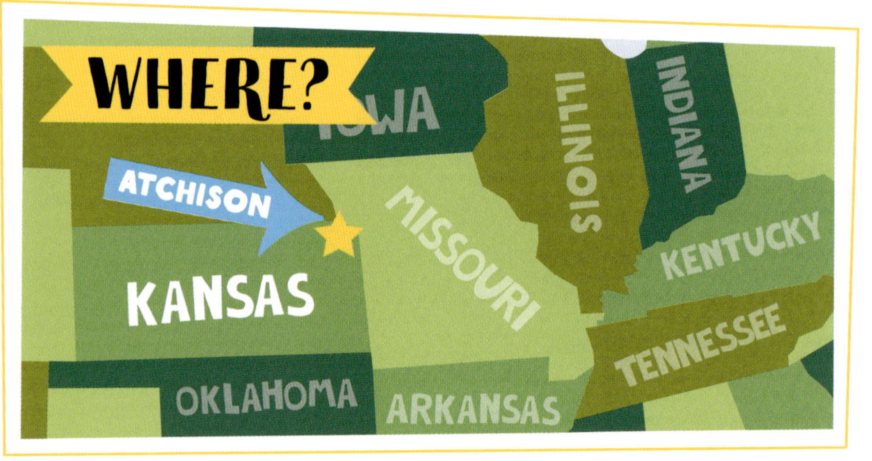

the years, Amelia would break many world flying records. She was the first female **pilot** to fly alone across the United States nonstop. She was also the first woman to cross the Atlantic Ocean alone. She set speed and distance records—and the women's record for flying the highest.

In 1937, Amelia tried to set one more record. She wanted to be the first woman to fly around the world. Near the end of the trip, her airplane disappeared over the ocean. No one knows for sure what happened to her. It's a mystery. What we do know is that Amelia helped women's rights and changed women's place in **aviation**. Her drive for adventure and strong will pushed the limits of what was possible, not just for women but for everyone.

Amelia's America

Amelia Mary Earhart was born July 24, 1897, in Atchison, Kansas. At that time, airplanes didn't exist. It wasn't until 1903, when Amelia was five years old, that Wilbur and Orville Wright built the first airplane and took the world's first-ever flight.

In the early 1900s, most people didn't go very far from home. If they had to travel, they walked or rode in a horse and buggy.

JUMP IN THE THINK TANK

When Amelia Earhart was growing up, many people thought women shouldn't be pilots. Were you ever told you couldn't do something? What did you do about it?

The gasoline-powered car was invented in 1886, but cars were expensive. A person could take a train across the United States or a boat across the ocean, but those trips took days or weeks.

When Amelia was growing up, many women stayed home with their families. Most women who worked outside the home were teachers, housekeepers, or salesclerks in shops. But these weren't jobs Amelia wanted. She wanted a different kind of career. She also didn't know if she wanted to get married.

> "Women, like men, should try to do the impossible. And when they fail, their failure should be a challenge to others."

When most girls and women were wearing dresses, Amelia preferred pants. She kept her hair short. It was hard for Amelia because she wasn't what people thought a woman should be.

Amelia had to make her own path to follow. Her journey would be a big adventure and would help all the women who came after her fulfill their dreams.

WHEN?

1886	1897	1903
The gasoline-powered car is invented.	Amelia Mary Earhart is born in Atchison, Kansas.	Wilbur and Orville Wright fly the first airplane.

CHAPTER 2
THE EARLY YEARS

Growing Up in Kansas

Amelia had one younger sister, Grace Muriel, who was nicknamed Pidge. Amelia had a nickname, too—Meelie. Their father, Edwin, was a lawyer for the railroad. He had to travel for work. Amelia and her sister often stayed with their mother's parents. Their grandparents had a nice large house, and the girls were comfortable there.

In 1904, Amelia and her family went to the St. Louis World's Fair. Seven-year-old Amelia was fascinated by the roller coaster. She wanted to ride it, but her mother said it was too dangerous.

Back at home, her uncle helped her build a roller coaster of her own. Amelia sat in a small crate at the top of a wooden track. The track started at the top of the toolshed and dropped to the ground. The crate slid down the crackling wooden track. Suddenly, it jumped off the track, flew through the air, and crashed. Amelia's dress was torn, and her lip was bruised. But Amelia didn't care. She had just done something she didn't think was possible. Her homemade roller coaster made her feel like she was flying!

Earhart Family Tree

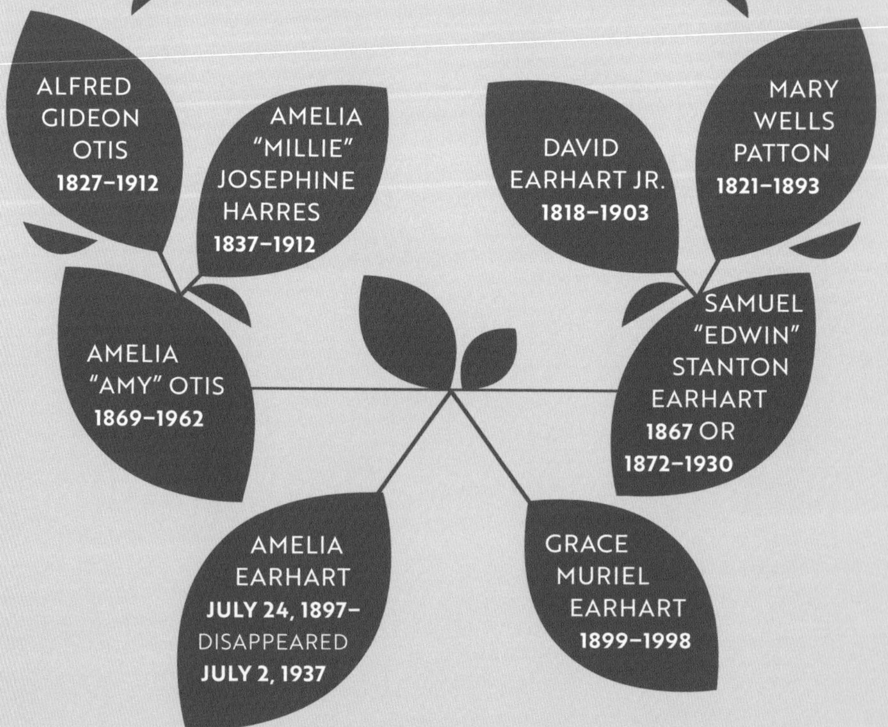

In 1908, she saw her first plane at the Iowa State Fair. Young Amelia wasn't impressed!

> "It was a thing of **rusty wire and wood** and looked not at all interesting."

What she didn't know was that a few years later, that rusty wire and wood plane that didn't look so interesting would change her entire life. Soon, she'd really get to fly—in her very own airplane!

JUMP IN THE THINK TANK

Have you ever moved homes? What were some good things about moving? What were the challenges? If you've never moved, where would you want to live and why?

On the Move

Amelia's life as a teenager was difficult. Edwin Earhart never made enough money to fully support his family. He changed jobs often, and the family moved many times. By the time she was in high school, Amelia had lived in Kansas, Iowa, Minnesota, and Illinois!

Amelia was unhappy at her new high school in Chicago, Illinois. In her free time, she collected

newspaper articles in a scrapbook. The articles talked about women in interesting jobs. Even at a young age, Amelia wanted to change the world's view of women.

When she graduated from high school, Amelia attended **junior college** in Pennsylvania. She played field hockey, enjoyed music, and was elected to the honor board. In 1917, on a school break, Amelia went to Toronto, Canada, where her sister was studying. There, Amelia saw injured soldiers returning from World War I. She wanted to do whatever she could to help the soldiers, so she decided to leave the junior college and become a nurse's aide. She even went back to school to become a

doctor. But after a few classes, she changed her mind and dropped out.

Amelia didn't know what she wanted to do. The year was 1920. Something big was waiting for her, but what was it?

WHEN?

1908 — Amelia sees a Wright brothers plane.

1914 — World War I begins in Europe.

1916 — Amelia graduates from high school.

1917 — Amelia leaves junior college to become a nurse's aide.

CHAPTER 3

AMERICA'S SUPER GIRL

The Show that Changed Everything

On December 28, 1920, Amelia and her father went to an air show in Long Beach, California. Amelia and her parents had moved to California earlier that year. A pilot named Frank Hawks was giving 10-minute airplane rides. So, Amelia took a ride in his plane. It was her first airplane ride ever. Right then, Amelia knew exactly what she wanted to do.

1920 was a good year for women. They had finally gained the right to vote.

MYTH & FACT

MYTH: Amelia Earhart was the first woman pilot.

FACT: While Amelia did a lot of things first, she wasn't the first woman pilot. In 1911, Harriet Quimby became the first female licensed pilot in the United States.

Women everywhere were learning that if they took chances, they could do the things they wanted. If Amelia wanted to be a pilot, nothing could stop her.

Amelia got to work! A week after her first flight, she took her first flying lesson. Her teacher was Mary Anita "Neta" Snook—one of the first women in history to have her own flight school. Amelia's father helped pay for the flying lessons. They cost a dollar a minute—that was a lot of money at the time. If Amelia wanted more than one lesson a week, she would need to get a job.

> **JUMP IN THE THINK TANK**
>
> When Amelia Earhart dreamed of flying, she took small jobs to make money. If you wanted flying lessons and an airplane, what kinds of jobs would you do?

Neta also taught Amelia to drive a car. Amelia was able to get a job driving a gravel truck for a construction company. She also worked as an office assistant, photographer, and typist.

Amy Earhart agreed to help her daughter with the extra money she needed. By the time she turned 25, Amelia could finally afford to purchase her own plane. She painted it yellow and named it the *Canary*.

Chasing Adventure

When Amelia first started flying, there weren't real airports or runways. Amelia crashed a few times. She had her own personal sense of style. She liked to wear pants and a scarf knotted at her neck. She kept her hair short, like other female **aviators**. Other pilots wore leather jackets, so Amelia bought one.

On December 15, 1921, Amelia finally earned her pilot's license. While she was learning to fly, her boyfriend asked her if she wanted to get married. Amelia said no. Her heart belonged only to flying.

In 1922, Amelia broke her first world record. She was the first woman to fly above 14,000 feet. Then, in 1923, she became the 16th woman ever to receive an **international** pilot's license.

Amelia was doing great things as a pilot, but she was having trouble paying her bills. The airplane and lessons cost too much. Her parents were also getting a divorce, which meant that they would no longer be married.

Amelia decided it was time for a change. In 1924, she sold the *Canary* and another plane she owned. She bought a yellow car, and she and her mother drove to Boston, where her sister lived. There, Amelia became a teacher and a social worker. She helped start a women's group for pilots. She flew planes in her free time, but it wasn't enough. Amelia wanted to fly all the time.

WHEN?

Amelia sees an air show in California.

1920

Amelia begins taking flying lessons.

1921

Amelia becomes the first woman to fly higher than 14,000 feet.

1922

Amelia earns an international pilot's license.

1923

CHAPTER 4

OVERNIGHT STARDOM

Amelia, Transatlantic Traveler

George Palmer Putnam was a publisher and a good businessman. In 1927, he published a book about a pilot named Charles Lindbergh. Lindbergh's nickname was "Lucky Lindy." The book was about Lucky Lindy's **solo** flight across the ocean from New York to Paris. The trip was the first solo, nonstop **transatlantic** flight anyone had ever tried.

The book about Lindbergh was a huge hit. George wanted to sell another book. He wanted to find a woman who could make a similar trip across the ocean. He heard that Amelia Earhart would be perfect for the job.

Amelia was excited to go on the flight, but she wasn't the pilot. Wilmer Stultz flew the plane. Louis Gordon was the copilot and mechanic. Amelia was a passenger. The flight from

Newfoundland to South Wales took 20 hours and 40 minutes.

Afterward, Amelia was a celebrity as the first woman ever to cross the Atlantic Ocean in an airplane! The newspapers called her "Lady Lindy" after Charles Lindbergh. But in an interview, Amelia said she felt like she was a bag of potatoes in the plane. She wanted to make the trip alone someday.

Amelia and George Putnam became close friends. He knew how to help her make money from her popularity. Over the next few years, Amelia worked very hard. She gave speeches, wrote a book, and designed luggage for travelers. Amelia also created a women's clothing line. George became her manager. Together, they looked for a way to make Amelia even more famous.

JUMP IN THE THINK TANK

How would you feel if you were Amelia, and you wanted to be a pilot but became famous for being a passenger instead?

Lady Lindy

In 1928, Amelia wrote a book about the transatlantic trip called *20 Hrs., 40 Min.: Our Flight in the Friendship*. It was named after how long the flight took. The book explained how the plane, called *Friendship*, took off in secret. It also talked about all the problems the crew had.

Amelia was surprised by how much attention she was getting. She knew she'd been asked to travel because she was a woman. In fact, the two men on the trip were paid. Amelia was not. What she didn't realize was how important the trip was for women everywhere. She was a role model. Women were excited that she'd done such a dangerous flight.

> "Flying might not be **all plain sailing . . .** but the fun of it is worth the price."

Cosmopolitan magazine asked her to write articles for them about aviation. At the time, flight in America was changing. Airplanes were becoming a safer, more normal way to travel. Soon, anyone could be a passenger. Amelia's articles made other women want to fly.

In her heart, Amelia never felt like she deserved the fame she'd gotten as a passenger in the *Friendship*. She wanted to be the pilot and do something really big and special. So, Amelia signed up for an airplane race.

Lindbergh flies solo across the Atlantic Ocean.

1927

Amelia is the first female passenger on a transatlantic flight.

1928

WHEN?

CHAPTER 5

AMELIA RISING

Flying High

In 1929, the Great Depression hit the United States. People lost jobs and had less money. Air travel was expensive. Still, people wanted to try it. At first, most of the passengers were men. Women seemed to be afraid to get into an airplane. Amelia Earhart wanted to convince women that flying was safe. One of her articles for *Cosmopolitan* magazine was called "Is It Safe for You to Fly?" The answer was, "Yes!"

> "Ours is the commencement of a flying age, and I am happy to have popped into existence at a period so interesting."

Amelia hoped that someday people would fly places instead of driving or taking trains. She worked with her friend Eugene Vidal, another pilot, on a new airline. Charles Lindbergh helped, too. They called the airline Transcontinental Air Transport. At first, the airline didn't do well. But Amelia's ideas and articles helped make people, especially women, believe that air travel was safe.

Amelia was happy, but she still wanted more. She loved a challenge. She also liked having her name in the newspaper. The Women's Air Derby was an airplane race from Santa Monica, California, to Cleveland, Ohio. In 1929, Amelia signed up and bought a new plane—a red Lockheed Vega. Nineteen women pilots started the eight-day race. Fifteen crossed the finish line. Amelia came in third place.

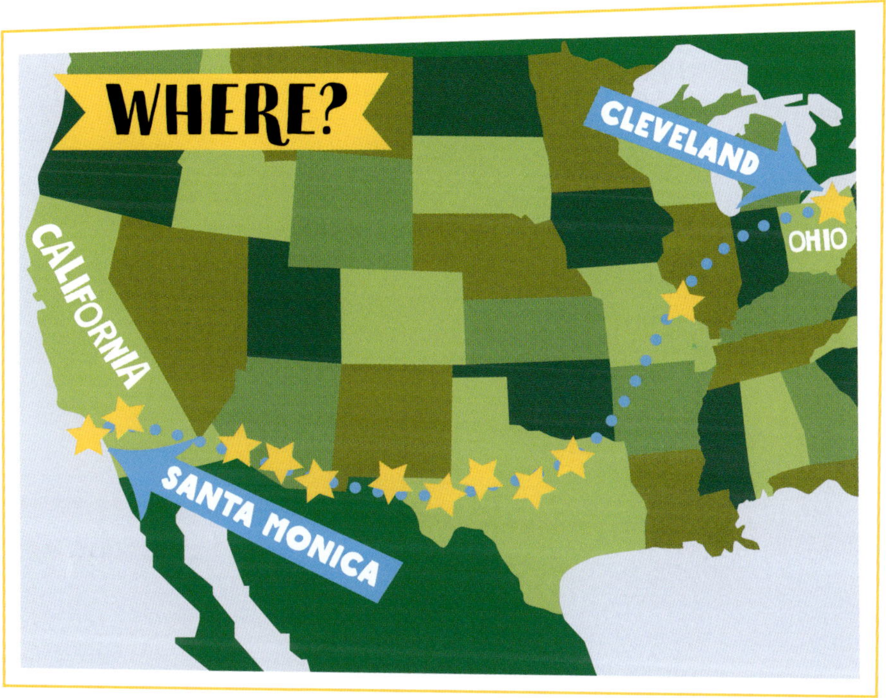

The race was difficult for all the pilots, but it was exciting! About 18,000 people came to watch the end of the race. That meant a lot more people were becoming interested in airplanes and flying. In 1930, Amelia broke yet another record: the women's flight speed record of 181 miles per hour. Everyone was watching to see what she would do next.

Life on the Ground

After the Women's Air Derby, Amelia and a group of female pilots formed a group called the Ninety-Nines. It was named for the number of women who started the **organization**. A year later, Amelia became the group's president.

The organization helped teach women to be pilots and set up **scholarships** to pay for some of their lessons.

In 1931, Amelia made a big change in her life. She decided to get married even though for years she had said she wouldn't. Amelia's father had died after the air derby. Amelia needed to help support her mother and sister. Her manager, George Putnam, had become her best friend. He proposed to her six times before she finally agreed.

JUMP IN THE THINK TANK

Think of an adventure you'd like to take someday. Where would you go? What would you do? Who would you invite to come with you?

Marriage was a difficult choice for Amelia. She worried that if she got married, she might not be able to follow her dreams or make her own decisions. George assured her that would not be the case. He knew how to make money during the Great Depression when others were struggling. If they got married, the money he made could also help her family. Before the wedding, Amelia gave George a letter. It said that if they weren't happy in a year, they'd get divorced. He agreed.

After she was married, Amelia went on to break more speed and flight records. It was never enough. She was hungry for adventure. She liked being famous, and her husband knew how to help her do that. Amelia and George started planning another trip—it would be a new world record!

WHEN?

1929	1930	1931
Amelia races in an air derby and helps start the Ninety-Nines.	Amelia sets the women's flight speed record of 181 mph.	Amelia marries George Putnam.

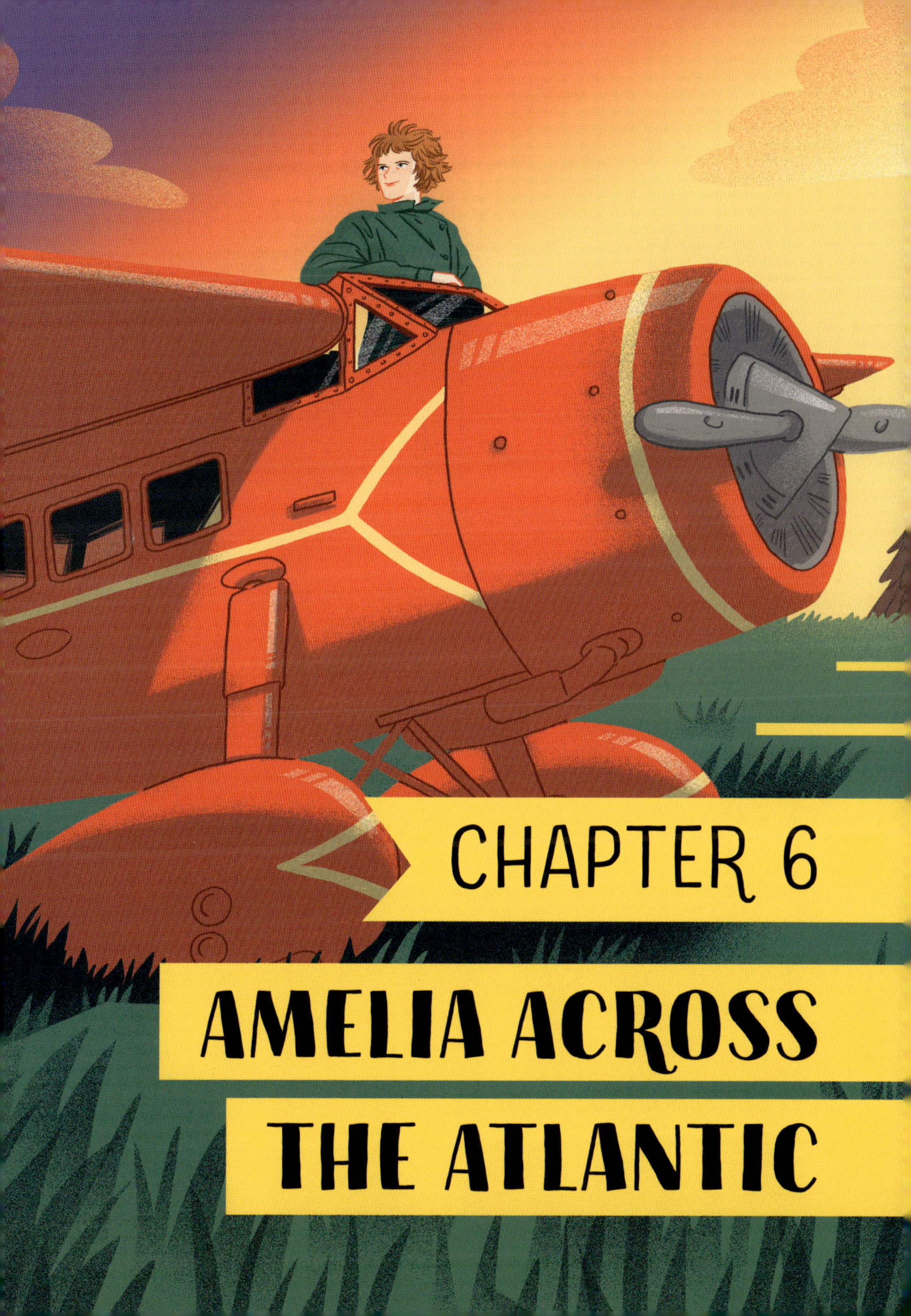

CHAPTER 6

AMELIA ACROSS THE ATLANTIC

Amelia Takes Off!

Amelia planned her exciting solo transatlantic flight in secret. She knew other women were planning the same trip and wanted to beat them to it. A friend of hers pretended to borrow her plane for a trip. He was actually giving it a tune-up so it would be ready for its record flight, with Amelia in the pilot's seat.

Finally, Amelia's red Lockheed Vega was ready to go. She called the plane *Old Bessie*. If all went well, she would be the first woman—and second person ever—to fly solo across the Atlantic. Her friends helped her fly the plane from New Jersey to St. Johns, Newfoundland, and on to Harbour Grace, Newfoundland, so Amelia could save her strength for her own flight.

On May 20, 1932, she climbed into her **cockpit**. This was the anniversary of the record flight Charles Lindbergh made five years earlier. She

would celebrate his anniversary with her own flight. *Old Bessie* took off over the ocean. Amelia's plane carried 420 gallons of gas and 20 gallons of oil. In case she got hungry, Amelia had chicken soup to eat along the way.

Amelia planned to land in Paris, just like Lindbergh did, but there were strong winds, and it was icy. The **altimeter** she used to tell how high she was flying broke. Amelia knew she would have to land soon—but where?

Lady Lindy Lands

The flight was bouncy, but Amelia held to her course. She managed to get *Old Bessie* high enough to fly safely for a while, but then more ice and rain came. Suddenly, the controls froze and the plane went into a spin. *Old Bessie* was in trouble. Amelia was an expert pilot. She was able to get things under control and fly safely.

A few hours later, she realized there was a gas leak. Fuel was dripping down her neck.

> "In my life I had come to realize that when things were going very well indeed it was just the time to anticipate trouble."

JUMP IN THE THINK TANK

What would you say if Amelia Earhart landed her airplane in your backyard?

It was time to land. She'd crossed the Atlantic, just like she'd planned, but landing in Paris was no longer an option. Amelia landed her plane in a farmer's field in Londonderry, Northern Ireland, and later said that she frightened the cows there. The trip took 14 hours and 56 minutes.

Amelia Earhart was famous before, but now she was more popular than ever.

Her first Atlantic crossing as a passenger was a memory. This time, she didn't feel like a sack of potatoes. She was the pilot! Amelia was awarded the Distinguished Flying Cross by the United States Congress for her record-setting flight. She also got the National Geographic Society's Gold Medal from President Herbert Hoover.

Amelia Earhart would be remembered forever for this historic trip. She could have stopped and rested. But she continued to work for women's causes and set more world records. Amelia was not done yet. She had even bigger dreams.

Amelia flies solo nonstop across the Atlantic.

1932

Amelia breaks her record for solo transatlantic flight.

1933

WHEN?

CHAPTER 7

MYSTERIOUS DISAPPEARANCE

The Final Record

Early in 1936, Amelia Earhart began planning her next big flight—and her last world record. She would fly around the world! Other people had already done this, but Amelia wanted to follow the **equator**. Her 29,000-mile route would be extremely challenging.

> "The lure of flight is the lure of beauty."

Lockheed Aircraft built Amelia an airplane called an Electra. The plane was originally meant to carry passengers, but it was changed for Amelia's flight. It had extra fuel tanks and the best radio equipment available.

On March 17, 1937, Amelia and her crew—Fred Noonan, Harry Manning, and Paul Mantz—flew from California to Hawaii. But they never started the second leg of the trip. During takeoff, the **landing gear** failed. Both **propellers** hit the ground as the plane skidded on its belly. The flight was canceled.

Only Amelia and Fred, her **navigator**, wanted to try again, so they made a few changes. They got rid of some equipment they didn't need. They also decided to fly in the opposite direction this time. On May 19, the plane was ready. Two days later, they left California for Miami. Then, it

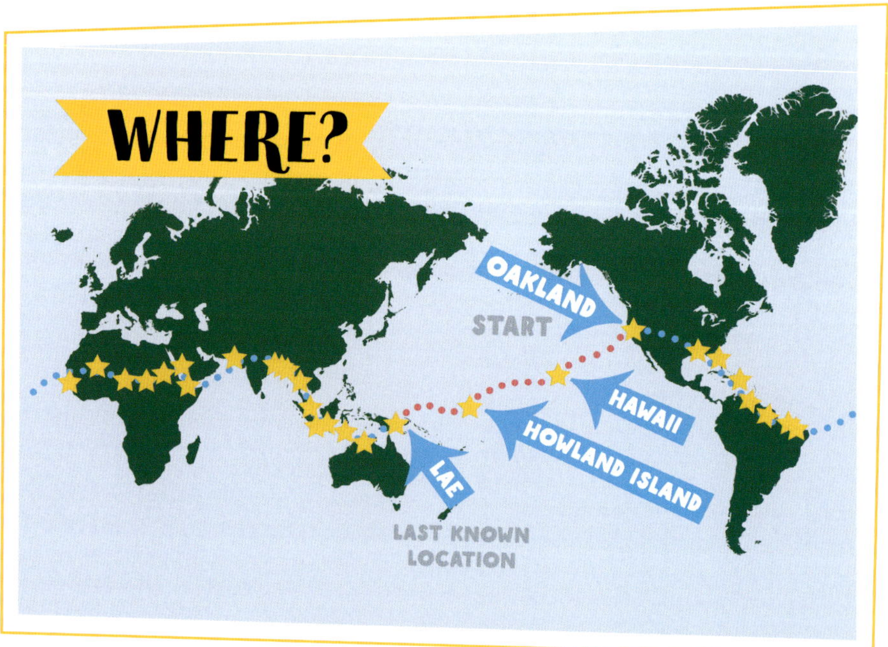

took a little over a month to fly from Miami to Lae, New Guinea, with a few stops between.

On July 2, 1937, Amelia took off for Howland Island in the Pacific. Fourteen hours and 15 minutes into the trip, the **Coast Guard** got a message from Amelia. It said the weather was cloudy and she couldn't find the island. The Coast Guard sent up smoke. She didn't see it. Amelia's message to them, sent at 8:43 a.m., was the last she ever sent. Amelia Earhart was lost.

Amelia, the Pioneer

No one knows what happened next. Some people think the Electra crashed. Other people think Amelia and Fred landed on another island and were **castaways**. No one heard from Amelia Earhart ever again. There were many search parties after she disappeared. On July 19, 1937, Amelia and Fred were declared lost at sea. Two years later, Amelia Earhart was finally pronounced dead.

In 1940, workers on Nikumaroro Island found a skull and 13 bones. At first, scientists thought the bones were from a man. Then, the bones were lost. Years later, in 2018, a scientist studied the report of the bones and determined they were from a woman. The scientist thought the bones must be from Amelia Earhart, but this was never proven true.

There are many more theories about Amelia's disappearance. Some people think she was secretly an American spy who was captured by

America's enemies. A few people think aliens abducted her. Others think she went into hiding in New Jersey. Today, people are still wondering what happened to Amelia Earhart and Fred Noonan that day. And yet, nothing definite has ever been found—not her plane, or a crash site.

Amelia's **legacy** is shadowed by the mystery of what happened to her on that last flight. But the many

JUMP IN THE THINK TANK

You've learned about what some people think happened to Amelia Earhart. What do you think happened to her?

things she did during her life are more important than how she died. She was a **pioneer** in flight who set many records for women pilots. She worked for equal rights for women. She inspired girls to dream big. She was a role model. Amelia Earhart was an American hero.

WHEN?

1937: Amelia flies around the globe and disappears.

1939: Amelia is pronounced dead.

1968: Amelia is honored in the National Aviation Hall of Fame.

1973: Amelia is honored in the National Women's Hall of Fame.

2015: A crater on the moon is named after Amelia Earhart.

CHAPTER 8

SO. . .WHO WAS AMELIA EARHART?

Challenge Accepted!

We've learned a lot about Amelia Earhart's life and dreams. It's time to test your knowledge. Here's a who, what, when, where, why, and how quiz. Flip back in the text if you need help finding the answers. What do you remember?

1 Where was Amelia born?

→ A Los Angeles, California
→ B Cincinnati, Ohio
→ C Atchison, Kansas
→ D Boston, Massachusetts

2 What was Amelia's childhood nickname?

→ A Meelie
→ B Amy
→ C Pidge
→ D High Flyer

3 **What job *didn't* Amelia have while trying to make money for flying lessons?**

- A Photographer
- B Truck driver
- C Typist
- D Chef

4 **What color was the *Canary*, Amelia's first airplane?**

- A Green
- B Yellow
- C Red
- D Orange

5 **What role did Amelia have in the 1928 flight across the Atlantic Ocean?**

- A Pilot
- B Passenger
- C Navigator
- D Flight attendant

6 **In what place did Amelia finish in the 1929 Women's Air Derby race?**

→ A First

→ B Third

→ C Fifth

→ D Eighth

7 **Where did Amelia land in 1932 when she flew solo across the Atlantic Ocean?**

→ A A farmer's field in Ireland

→ B The airport in London

→ C A runway in Paris

→ D A street in Scotland

8 **What flight world record did Amelia try to earn in 1937?**

→ A First woman in space
→ B First woman to fly solo across the United States
→ C First woman to be awarded the Distinguished Flying Cross
→ D First woman to fly around the globe at the equator

9 **Why did Amelia's first around-the-world flight fail?**

→ A The plane ran out of gas
→ B She got sick
→ C The plane crashed at takeoff
→ D The weather was bad

10 **What island was Amelia supposed to land on when she disappeared?**

→ A Howland Island
→ B Hawaii
→ C Puerto Rico
→ D Japan

ANSWERS: 1. C; 2. A; 3. D; 4. B; 5. B; 6. B; 7. A; 8. D; 9. C; 10. A

Our World

Amelia's life changed the world. Amelia was a great pilot and an example of how women can do whatever they dream of doing. Let's look at a few things that are different today because of Amelia Earhart.

→ When Amelia and the other female pilots formed the Ninety-Nines, there were only 117 registered women pilots. Today there are about 30,000 pilots who are women. There are also more than 155 different chapters of the Ninety-Nines. Next time you fly, be sure to check who is in the airplane's cockpit!

→ Amelia was a champion for women's causes. She wanted women to have as many choices as men, in a time when that wasn't the case. Not only did she fight for the rights of female pilots, she fought for all women. She encouraged women to travel on airplanes, to have a career if they wanted one, and to live big adventures.

→ Amelia challenged women to think about careers that were usually only held by men. Women started signing up for more math, science, and engineering classes. Today, studying STEM (science, technology, engineering, and math) is very popular for both boys and girls.

JUMP IN THE THINK TANK FOR MORE!

Amelia Earhart never gave up on her goals. Let's think about what we can learn from her.

- → Amelia never lost sight of her dreams. Who are some other people you can think of who never gave up on their dreams?
- → If Amelia asked you which subject you like best—science, technology, engineering, or math—what would you tell her? Why?
- → Flying an airplane was Amelia's favorite thing to do. What is your favorite thing to do?

Glossary

altimeter: An instrument used for showing how high a person or an airplane is above the ground

aviation: Anything that relates to airplanes or other machines that fly

aviator: A person who flies an aircraft

castaway: A person who is stranded on an island or drifting at sea after a shipwreck or accident

Coast Guard: The branch of the United States military that enforces laws at sea and protects the country's waterways

cockpit: The area of the plane where the pilot sits at the controls

equator: The imaginary line that that surrounds Earth at its widest part

international: Something that involves many countries

junior college: A school that offers classes for two years after high school

landing gear: The parts under the airplane that are used for takeoff and landing

legacy: Something a person leaves behind for which they are remembered

navigator: The person on an airplane or ship who plans the route and keeps track of where the plane or ship is on the map

organization: A group of people with a common goal

pilot: The person who controls the aircraft

pioneer: A person who is the first to do something

propeller: A turning blade that helps push or pull an airplane forward

scholarship: Money that is given to a student to help pay for school

solo: By oneself, alone

transatlantic: Having to do with crossing the Atlantic Ocean

Bibliography

"Amelia Earhart, 1897-1937." PBS.org. Accessed March 3, 2020. pbs.org/wgbh/americanexperience/features/earhart-timeline/.

"Amelia Earhart." AmeliaEarhart.com. Accessed April 3, 2020. ameliaearhart.com.

"Amelia Earhart." Biography.com. Accessed March 8, 2020. biography.com/explorer/amelia-earhart.

"Amelia Earhart Biography." NotableBiographies.com. Accessed March 1, 2020. notablebiographies.com/Du-Fi/Earhart-Amelia.html.

"Amelia Earhart." Barron Hilton Pioneers of Flight Gallery, Smithsonian National Air and Space Museum. Accessed April 3, 2020. pioneersofflight.si.edu/content/amelia-earhart-0.

Earhart, Amelia. *20 Hrs., 40 Min.: Our Flight in the Friendship*. Washington, D.C.: National Geographic Society, 2003.

Earhart, Amelia. *Last Flight: The World's Foremost Woman Aviator Recounts, in Her Own Words, Her Last, Fateful Flight*. New York: Putnam, 1937.

Fleming, Candace. *Amelia Lost: The Life and Disappearance of Amelia Earhart*. (New York: Schwartz & Wade, 2011.)

Harkin, Sofia. "Amelia Earhart Biography for Kids." Lottie.com. March 9, 2015. lottie.com/blogs/strong-women/18992639-amelia-earhart-biography-for-kids.

Jones, Victoria Garrett. *Amelia Earhart: A Life in Flight*. New York: Sterling, 2009.

Karbo, Karen. "How Amelia Earhart navigated the skies and society." *In Praise of Difficult Women: Life Lessons from 29 Heroines Who Dared to Break the Rules*. Washington, D.C.: National

Geographic Society, 2018. nationalgeographic.com/culture/2019/01/Amelia-Earhart-praise-difficult-women-book-excerpt/.

"More Stories of Amelia Earhart." Amelia Earhart Birthplace Museum. Accessed March 14, 2020. ameliaearhartmuseum.org/AmeliaEarhart/AEMoreStories.htm.

"Photo sparks renewed interest in Abington's Amelia Earhart." *Penn State News,* accessed March 14, 2020. news.psu.edu/story/474077/2017/07/06/campus-life/photo-sparks-renewed-interest-abingtons-amelia-earhart.

Rich, Doris L. *Amelia Earhart: A Biography.* Washington, D.C.: Smithsonian Books, 1989.

Stone, Tanya Lee. *Amelia Earhart: A Photographic Story of a Life.* New York: DK Publishing, 2007.

About the Author

STACIA DEUTSCH is a *New York Times* best-selling author and has written more than 300 children's books. She started her career with the award-winning chapter book series Blast to the Past. Her résumé includes popular ghostwritten mysteries in addition to junior movie tie-in novels for summer blockbuster films like *The Smurfs* and the Hotel Transylvania series. Her new books include the Spirit Riding Free series and *Girls Who Code: The Friendship Code*. And, yes, Stacia is also a reform rabbi. Find her at **StaciaDeutsch.com**, **@staciadeutsch**, and **Facebook.com/staciadeutsch**.

About the Illustrator

PEARL LAW is an illustrator, zine-maker, comic artist, and visual recorder. She loves to play around with visual wit and exploring the best narrative possible through problem-solving, solid line work, and nice bold colors. Much of her work takes inspiration from humor, literature, history, and behavioral observations. Pearl graduated from University of the West of England in the UK with a degree in illustration. She now lives in Hong Kong, and fantasizes about living in a cottage someday.